Kady Karinas

FLYING BEYOND THE STARS

A Startling Post Death Experience and Return

Kady Karinas

Flying Beyond The Stars. Copyright
©2019 by Kady Karinas

All rights reserved. No part of this book may be reproduced or transmitted in any form or by any means without written permission from the author.
ISBN: - 9781798945780

Lady Karinas   *Flying Beyond The Stars*

Dedication

I would like to dedicate the content of this book if I may to my family and friends; those I will be leaving behind when my time here is finally done and to those too who wait to welcome me home into an amazing perspicacious spirit world that I found to be a loving safe reality beyond this life.

The purpose of writing this book is to produce a record of the astonishingly true event that took place for me on a lovely beautiful dawn morning.

This is what I know now... Once we fulfill our obligations towards our own soul on this biological earth 'forever is ours... as it always was!'

Chapters

Dedication	5
Introduction	9
Startling Departure	11
Through the Vortex	22
About Turned	23
Gift from Heaven-A New Husband	34
Heart Sent from Heaven	46
Lonán's Extraordinary Events	47
Unforgettable Happenings	49
The Spirals	59
Help from A Dying Uncle	61
Angels in Disguise	66
Cross in the Clouds	70
Foretold in Every Detail	71
Angel Music	79
Guardian Angel	81
Residue of a Heavenly Visit	87
Warning from Heaven!	89
Merging Souls- A Love That Refused To Die!	94
Mi Cariño	96
Final Thoughts.	102

[Please note the differences between U.K and U.S spellings, i.e. U.S = 'color, traveling, realize, neighbor, honor etc.,' but in the U.K = it's 'colour, travelling and realise, neighbour honour, etc.,' Due to my association with both countries I do tend to mix both forms of grammar. Thank you.]

~~~~~~~~~~~~~~~~~~~~~~

~~~~~~~~~~~~~~~~~~~

This 'angel/cross image' {above} was seen high up in the trees of a lovely little church and its grounds but it was only noticed on examination of the photograph we had taken of the church which looked so pretty in the sunlight.

~~~~~~~~~~~~~~~~~~~~~

[There are many mysteries within the universe of the Great Consciousness we will never discover while we remain in the hold of our biological bodies held within the biological planet we call earth...

... I died 'had an OBE or as I prefer a DRE.. 'a dying retuning event' and travelled through and beyond the stars while in a different composition of form to find my way home where I experienced the revealing of many mysteries!]

Introduction

By writing this book I hope to help alleviate the fear that many of us have of dying. Having shot out of my body when it stopped breathing I found myself in another dimension that was 'far more real than life here!' Initially the vortex I entered was dark but its darkness wasn't scary or uncomfortable but rather it was 'soothing.'

This is a 'word for word' or rather a 'thought for thought' account as I thought my thoughts about what was happening to me inside my vortex after catapulting out of my body.

I do not to attempt to wrap the experience I write about up in any kind of religious theology because it was not that neither do I want to lesson religious or scientific study.

Although to my mind my experience was more phenomenal than any religious or scientific research or study could begin to rationalize simply because of its unknown quantity in their eyes and also because the physical cannot prove what is corporeal!

I use the word 'Angel' to describe the kindly beings who came to my aid simply for want of a better word.

My story happened one morning a few minutes after the stirrings of early dawn as I lay wide awake eagerly waiting to get on with my day because the earlier it got underway the sooner I would be home again...

... but my musings came to an abrupt end when I felt a crushing pain in my chest as if an elephant had stamped down on it, I then 'immediately catapulted' out of my body!

~~~~~~~~~~~~~~~~~~~~~~

Startling Departure

I'll be so tired by this evening; the excitement of going home today has most probably made me feel this restless. I want to be home in my own sweet little kitchen.

I want to see little Lohintzun's face light up when I give him his present and I'm looking forward to planting out those bulbs Celeste gave to me before I left for the Mediterranean.

A cup of coffee would be nice but I think I had better give it half an hour then I'll sneak downstairs and make myself one.

Oh no here we go again, my chest feels tight. I'll have to relax, 'go with it,' soon it will subside.

Coffee would have prevented this; as soon as it passes I'm going down that stairs whether he wakes up or not!

He has a way of making me feel guilty if I should dare to become unwell.

Oh... gosh! Wow! I've catapulted right out of my body!

I'm outside of my body and there's no pain. The pain has gone! I feel light free and new!

Its me on the bed, lifeless! That means dead but I'm not dead, I feel odd. Oh uh... where am I going?

Strange, I don't understand. I look serene down there but I'm here! It's odd but I feel good.

I'm part of the bedroom, I see it but I am not part of it! I like the 'feel of all this though!'

I see parts of the bedroom, the furniture. I'm aware of 'him' deeply asleep at my side, everything seems as it should be but 'I'm not as I should be!'

I want to stay, to watch over my dead body. I want to keep looking at my 'dear' self down there! Its 'my shell but what do I do now?

I know it doesn't matter what happens to my body now, it's dead!

I feel a little lost.

It's odd but this is me outside that body! This is who I am and it's all fine.

I feel peaceful; I know all is well, I know I will be ok... I am ok! I am still myself but more so!

There's something to my left... A grey puffy mist.

It's pulling me into it and through it into a tunnel! I'm inside the tunnel!

I'm moving forward!

I am not putting any effort into this so why am I flying?

I didn't decide to have my arms out in front of me either yet I can't see them. Everything is getting lighter and lighter.

All around me is becoming gently colourful and now even more colourful.

I see is a tiny pinprick of light up ahead. A sunny white gold sort of light. It's a long way off. It seems many thousands of miles away. I want to reach it.

This is not a tunnel anymore, it's a vortex enveloping me. I'm travelling through it so fast!

Something is chartering my progress! My trajectory seems to have been planned for me.

That light is getting larger. I want to know what's ahead but not yet awhile.

Someone is joining alongside of me!

I don't see him but I feel it's a he and he's travelling in the same direction as I.

He's keeping up with my speed but I'm moving too fast to look sideways.

I think he's here to help me along.

He seems to be here to give me a safe passage. He feels comforting. 'He's talking to me inside my head... telepathically!'

'Yes I know my body is dead and I know I am safe.' I know this already! I am alright, thank you.

His voice is beautiful. I know his voice, it's part of me but who is he? He feels like family. I'm talking to him with my mind!

Everything is so peaceful and brighter now.

That speck of light looks larger; it's getting larger as I get nearer; it's inviting and exciting.

I'm going to go through that light; it's an opening into or onto something.

Earth!?

It's an earth like planet!

It's huge, it's beautiful! Thrilling! Blue and pristine!

I'm coming...

'I am coming!'

I hear you. I can feel you! I am coming.

I've missed all of you so much; my late loved ones! I'm so happy!

I feel all your love for me; my family... my friends animals and birds.

I didn't know I was so cared about!
Loved!

Oh gosh... No! How could I have forgotten you both? How could I forget you?

I can't leave you. How will you both and little Lohintzun know where I have gone?

~~~~~~~~~~~~~~~~~~~~~~~

Celeste

How am I this close to you Celeste, my
daughter and my first born. I'm part of you!
I feel your thoughts as you slumber!

I feel your breath. I feel your soul within
me and
it's wonderful.

It's me, it's me your Mom but I have to
leave you

just for this point in time.
I am so sorry because I don't want to
leave you
I love you.
I am not far away.
I am dead but I am
far from being dead,
it's just my
physical body that is dead I am
within you, within your soul.

It's so beautiful. I love
you. I am really here
with you.
I feel you
within my own soul. I will
truly be part of you.
always
I h·ave to go
for now
but It's
not forever.
I Love You

~~~~~~~~

Ricard

I feel your breath. I feel your soul

within me. It's wonderful

It's me, it's me your Mom. I have to leave

you but

it's just for

this point in

time.

I am so sorry because I don't want

to leave you

I love you.

I am not far away. I am dead

but I am

far from being dead,

it is only my

physical body that is dead.

I am within you, within your soul. It's

beautiful. I love you.

I am really here with you

I feel you

within my soul.

I will truly be part of you.

always

I have to go; just for now

but it's not forever.

I Love You

Lohintzun

~~~~~~~~

My second born son.

I see you there, your almost inside the tunnel with me,

You're so far away, so little, so young.

Please don't cry, you must be quite unwell to cry for Mummy like this

but you don't yet know your Mummy won't be at home

waiting for you

to take you back to school with me on Monday.

Your longing for me is heartbreaking.
I am so sorry.
I do not want to come back

but

your sorrow is too hard for me to bear;

I need to be with you

to care for you.

'Your little soul cannot hear me my

love 'because your grief is too overwhelming for me to break

through to you.

Oh my gosh! How quickly I died!

I had no intention to do so!

I had no warning!

I am so sorry!

I Love You.

My children!

~~~~~~~~~~~~~~~~~~~~

Those are the thoughts that ran through my 'after physical consciousness' as I flew through my protective vortex.

I could still feel emotion as well as shock even though I was no longer a biological person!

I felt great love too as I travelled and as I travelled on through the vortex I was able 'astonishingly' to be part of my children's inner consciousness!'
I did not know how this was so but I accepted it as a normal thing to be doing!

[We are born into this world 'accepting ourselves and everything around us as normal' it was the same after catapulting out of my dead body... I accepted my new life's reality 'as normal!']

Through the Vortex

About midway through the vortex colours appeared the beautiful gentle colours of the spectrum which sadly I cannot reproduce.

Once inside the vortex I felt excitement and wonder but also a feeling of
'complete peace.'

About Turned

In the moment that I asked 'who will be able to care for my child now?' I heard the voice of my companion say within my consciousness 'this need not be your time, you decided!'

Immediately on hearing his words I was 'about turned speeding back the way I had come!

No longer could I see the light that had started off as a small dot in the distance and I knew I had to leave behind the loved ones 'humans as well as animals' who had shared their past earthly lives with me.

Then the vortex 'became dark as I sped back into my biological body' which was still able to receive me back!

I lay on there on the bed stunned in shock because I had been to Heaven and back; the dawn chorus was still going on and the bedroom felt the same yet I would never be the same again!

Gradually a sense of peace and joy came over me as I realized that the I 'the who I am' goes on just as my late loved ones who were once biological are still themselves and alive but in a different form of being!

In that moment of clarity I wanted to tell everyone.

I felt such an indescribable happiness and surety that has never left me despite all the ups and downs and woes of this existence.

In that moment I could still feel the non judgemental love of those I had left behind in a heavenly world I can only describe as 'a nirvana of immense consciousness.

Even though it's been many years since my DCB 'dying coming back experience' I recall everything vividly that happened within my vortex as well as the things I learned as I travelled through which had a huge significance for me, yet I know there are other things I forgot as soon as I was about turned.

[Everything that has biological life goes on but then changes on mortal physical demise 'as a butterfly metamorphoses from one form into another more beautiful form.']

However I have remembered this 'the character traits of integrity or lack of it that I allow myself to cultivate or follow in this life will automatically determine the level of existence I will experience within my post earth life. 'A reality that awaits us within our spirit's consciousness i.e... the quality of living our being will know 'when we finally vacate the biological body.'

I was so happy to discover the fact that every living creature that existed here in a biological life 'goes on' just as we do!

For me this discovery was 'is' wonderful to know this because I have loved and cared for quite a few animals and bird friends during my life here.

After I shot out of my physical self I felt so alive, full of the joie de vivre 'joy of life.'

I knew many amazing facts as I travelled through my vortex,' I do not know how I knew these things but I lost much of that knowledge as soon as I was about turned to find myself travelling back into my physical body.'

I have retained some of the 'knowing' I had inside my vortex such as knowing there are more experiences coming my way for me to work through so I can continue 'to grow my soul's understanding' before I leave this mortal life to take my place on the next level of experiences my spirit has to learn for its progression through an eternal existence.

I say 'us and we and our' in this context because I knew that part the knowledge I perceived was a 'collective knowing.'

On entering the safety of the vortex and for what seemed like a long time as I zoomed through I couldn't see anything outside of it until I was almost at its end when I saw space and planets and then 'a beautiful earth like world looming up right in front of me, looking very large!

I didn't like journeying back because the vortex became dark immediately I was 'about turned' whereas the vortex had been light beautiful and colourful beforehand!'

I was quite heartbroken at the thought of coming back to this world even though I had not wanted to die but I knew I couldn't leave my young child or have my young adult children facing grief and shock over my sudden death if I had the chance to return.

It seemed an age since I had exited my physical body but now it felt like it was just seconds and once back inside of it, it breathed beautifully!

I lay there on the bed in stunned shock for quite some time as I thought about everything that had happened while my partner lay sleeping at my side and as I turned to look at his face I wondered why or how it was that I hadn't felt any love or connection with him after I left my body as I had with my children?

Indeed as I looked down on my own lifeless body I did not look down at all upon this man I thought I adored even though I was aware of him lying at the side of my dead body but unknown to me he was in fact a person it was not good for anyone to interact with.

Nowadays I realise it may be that my spirit consciousness may have known this fact all along.

Yet I felt guilty for a long time about not feeling any connection with him after I left my dead body but this was a guilt misplaced because a while later I went on to discover what a dreadfully bad person this man was.

As time passed and as I got on with my life unusual events of a ghostly kind began to take place such as the night I was on my way back to bed and just about to slip eagerly back between the sheets as the night was really chilly when I saw the usual form of a distant relative standing at the foot of my bed looking as normal as always but then as I stared in utter wonderment this family member of mine without saying a word gently faded away before my very eyes!

Another strange event happened during one summer while I attended a rather interesting light hearted seminar.

I listened intently enjoying the words of the speaker when something at his feet caught my eye.

I looked down to that point where to my utter astonishment I saw my dear beloved dog but she had died more than twenty seven years previously!

Her black coat with the white ruff at her throat was beautiful and glossy!

I watched her chasing her tail in delight at the sight of me.

I stared at her for some time until right before my eyes she faded away!

I had loved that dog dearly.

I looked at the faces around me but it was obvious that no one else but me had seen her.

A few months later as I hurried through my kitchen area I hit my ankle quite awkwardly against a very old gas pipe protruding out from a skirting board as I attempted to avoid a clothes airer.

It hurt but I was tired and it was late in the evening and I had other things to think about so I ignored the pain as much as I could. I thought it would probably be better by the morning and it was.

I spent the next day trekking around Calais France in the company of one hundred children and four teachers so it was a relief to be back at home at the end of the day.

By now my ankle was badly swollen but I had the weekend all to myself; ample time to rest I thought however it hurt so much that I decided to sleep downstairs on the sofa which I did quite happily and fell asleep.

I awoke at five am to see my late mother standing between the wall and the back of the sofa 'a physical impossibility as the sofa was flush to the wall' but there was Mom leaning over the arm of the sofa lifting her arms through my leg!

I stared in awe as she kept trying to lift my leg until I felt a sudden pain in my ankle then the penny dropped.

I realized my ankle was hurting because it was stuck in a gap between the sofa's cushion and sofa's end so I got myself into a sitting position bent forward and gently lifted my foot with both of my hands as my beloved mother looked on.

As soon as this was done my beloved Mom began to fade away! I felt a great feeling of love emanating from her as she faded from me but I was longing for her to stay!

I cried out pleadingly 'please don't go' but as the words left my lips my dear Mom slowly disappeared.

My ankle was very swollen and painful but I didn't care all I could think of was Mother and the love I felt coming from her.

I desperately wanted her to come back, if only for one more moment but I was so happy that

Mom had come to visit me from heaven or wherever the home or level of her reality was and what it is actually called.

Thinking back on this experience brings tears of longing to my eyes, I miss her so much.

My next experience was 'a dream.'

In this dream I drove home along a country road I knew well having driven along it frequently.

It was very late at night when all of a sudden I saw a huge brown rat run out of a hedge and under the wheel of my car. I woke up knowing I had killed it.

The following night I drove along that exact same country road when just as in my dream the previous night a huge brown rat ran out of a hedge at the same spot as in my dream and got caught under the wheel of my car.

I would have avoided it but it happened too quickly for me to do anything.

I stopped the car but there was nothing I could do for the poor animal.

I know it was just a rat but it saddened me to think I caused the little creature pain.

I failed to see the point of why I was given the dream at the time because I couldn't have done anything differently.

I suppose though in hindsight I must admit I had completely forgotten about the dream as I drove home that night; if only I had remembered I would have driven past that spot more carefully and slowly.

Another time just as I was about to watch my usual afternoon movie as was my custom; I walked across the room towards my comfortable favourite solid flowery covered armchair to startlingly realize my dear late Mother was standing behind it!

This time I saw her through a veil of beautiful 'shimmering colours; colours of silvery blues pinks lilacs and white' she looked so lovely and so beautiful but as soon as I registered what I was seeing she began to fade away!

I blurted out 'oh Mom don't go' but by the time I finished the sentence she was gone!

I was so surprised and shocked yet utterly elated too by

having had the privilege of such a visitation so much so that I lost all interest in the afternoon film I had planned to watch!

~~~~~~~~~~~~~~~~~~~~

The lovely colours I saw around
my mother's spirit body
had the appearance of
a
'shimmering veil.'

KadyK 2019.

[The beautiful pale colours of this
spectrum
are similar to those I saw
surrounding the ghost of my
beloved late mother back in 2002]

~~~~~~~~~~~~~~~~~~~~

A Gift from Heaven ~
A New Husband!

Not long after my dear mother's second visit I was about to sit down to watch yet another afternoon film on the television 'again as was my custom before preparing the evening family meal' but before doing so I headed on into my bedroom to find the chocolate treat I kept in my bedside table drawer for such occasions.

On entering the room something to the right of me up in mid air caught my eye.

I looked up and it was as if someone had switched on a video or hologram right there in mid air!

I stared up at the scene in such surprise! I was utterly transfixed to the spot I stood on!

There in mid air I saw a long highly polished table. Around this table sat two women and four men.

At one end of the table sat a jovial silver haired man with striking blue eyes. A man of great presence.

I heard his sweet velvet voice as he kept his six friends enthralled by what he was saying which I couldn't quite understand but the scene was pleasant and exciting to watch. I stared enthralled in an uplifting sense of amazement then as quickly as it had appeared 'it was gone' as if some unseen hand had switched it off!

I felt disappointed and surprised that it had gone and so quickly!

I couldn't think of anything else but this experience for days afterwards and dared tell only one person about it; the advice I received was given with a smile and disbelieving laughter, I should see a doctor!'

Almost three weeks later I was enjoying a shopping trip in a small seaside town I had recently fallen in love with.

Having completed some purchases I made my way towards a café I liked only to find a notice on the door that said 'closed.

I hadn't noticed just how quickly the afternoon had passed even though I knew I had spent more time than usual over some of purchases but it had closed a little early; with a sense of resignation I shrugged my shoulders and made my way back to the car but as I walked I noticed my chest go tight, I found it difficult to get enough air into my lungs.

Finding it more and more difficult to breathe I reached into the pocket of my coat for my bronchodilator only to realise I had forgotten to bring it with me.

This oversight wouldn't have mattered so much if the café hadn't been closed because a cup of coffee and a short rest would have put me right.

[Coffee and 'bronchodilators contain a certain ingredient called Theophylline' which have the effect of relaxing the muscles of the lungs.]

I looked around me; I seemed to be the only person on the street until I saw someone walking hurriedly along on the opposite side of the road, he looked over at me but he must have thought I was drunk or something because he didn't come to my aid but carried on walking.

I managed to reach the outside wall of a building put down my shopping parcels and leaned back against the wall. I knew I had to stay calm and wait for the episode to pass.

I tried to stay calm but panic was beginning to set in so I closed my eyes said a prayer for help and then I realized I was leaning against the wall of a pretty little pub that was still open.

I remembered being told previously that this place sold the best coffee in town but I was brought up in an era that looked down on a female walking into a 'pub' unescorted so I thought 'oh gosh I can't walk in there alone Mom will turn in her grave so to speak!'

But I soon realised how ridiculous that reasoning was because I knew no one could be trapped in rotting bodies in graves or otherwise after death because I 'shot out of my physical body once it died and found myself already in the realms of the place Jesus called paradise and the robust consciousness of my energy was completely free of my biological body.'

I wasn't lying somewhere in purgatory. The shell of my dead biological body didn't matter one jot whatsoever because I was free of it! I was 'already a free being' able to think for myself and in my case 'a being able and willing to realise my earthly experience was for me to learn to grow in love and compassion for others in tough circumstances.

That was the job of work I was born to work through!

[Nowadays in my quiet moments I often wonder if the nuclear wars spoken of in those old ancient Hindu texts had actually wiped out forever much the earth's truth's and natural food sources 'foods we may know nothing of today.'

Wars don't work in the long run because they instil the idea that war is the only way to settle and take from others, sadly of course leaders 'the controlling ones who bend truth' do not wish to learn any other way.]

By now I was desperate for help because I had a little dog waiting back in the car for me.

No-one would know she was there because she was a very small black dog who just went to sleep on the back seat whenever I left her in the car as well as it being her practice to ignore any passers-by so I knew it would be difficult for anyone to notice her.

[That dog was such a sweet natured dear little 'rescued dog.' Sad to say her little body died the same week as we had beloved Lonán's funeral.] I was so desperate to get back to her that necessity spurred me into action.

I picked up my parcels of shopping and edged myself slowly around the corner of the building towards its doorway.

Having reached the door I rested up a moment as I gained the strength to push it open and as I did this I felt someone take my shopping from my hands then lead me to a chair.

My rescuer was a sweet woman with lovely long brown hair; she reminded me of one of my favourite aunts.

I hardly got my words out as I asked for two cups of coffee but she understood turned and rushed off in the direction of the bar.

This is when I realized she was actually a barmaid.

The establishment was packed; all eyes seemed to be on me for what seemed like an eternity. I didn't know where to look so I stared intently at the ashtray in front of me until my kindly barmaid was back at my side with the coffee.

I looked up and gave her a smile of thanks as she informed me that she would bring the second coffee to me as soon as I had finished the first.

I sipped that welcome coffee until the tightness in my chest gradually eased then I overheard a couple of guys at my side say they thought I looked like a heart stopper or words to that effect.

That was nice I smiled to myself until I heard the next part of the sentence 'but a bit of a schoolmistress type.'

Oh ok I thought, deflated then thought 'I liked being seen as a schoolmarm 'thank you' yet still feeling a little embarrassed I reached into my shopping bag where I found a newspaper I thought I could try to pretend to read...

... so lifting the spectacles that hung on a chain around my neck this is what I proceeded to do mindful of the fact that they would make me look even more like the schoolmarm type which I ...

... was in all practicality anyway because I recently started work at little Lohintzun's school helping out as a teachers assistant but I had not thought of myself as that type before.

After a while I glanced up from my newspaper and looked around tentatively, the room was packed full; people stood around for want of seating space.

To the right side of me I saw two women and four men sitting around a long highly polished table and there at one end of the table sat a pleasant genial silver haired man with striking blue eyes.

A man of great presence.

I listened to his light velvety voice as he kept his companions enthralled with his engaging story.

The scene was exact in every detail as I had seen in my bedroom up to the right of me almost three weeks beforehand!

Each person's face and voice around that table was exactly as I had seen and heard in what to me was a 'precognitive holographic vision!'

I stared at the scene in amazement until one of the women stared back at me in an overly enquiring manner. I looked away quickly feeling somewhat shamefaced for staring.

I continued to pretend to read until I felt well enough to get up and leave.

A few minutes later 'feeling a lot better' I stood up and was just about to pick up my shopping when I felt a hand on my left elbow and heard the voice of the silver haired man who had sat at the end of that long table a few moments previously ask if I would like him to carry my shopping to the door.

He noticed my distress earlier he said and so he wondered if he could help.

I looked up into those beautiful striking blue mesmerizing eyes of his and kindly handsome face and said yes instinctively!

This delightful man walked with me to my car where we chatted for a while but not long enough as I would have stayed there in his company forever.

I was so pleased when he asked to see me again!

Eventually this wonderful man 'Lonán' and I married!

I loved him dearly but sad to say we had far too little time together before he fell ill.

He once told me that he believed his late wife 'Clara' who had died twenty two years previously had looked down from Heaven and brought us together 'a lovely thing for him to say I thought.'

When I leave this world, I just want to be with that little bit of him that belongs to me because I know the other part of his heart belongs to Clara.

Heavenly love is 'not a named love but rather a soul love.' We have or find more than one soul love once we leave this world.

Each love is different 'taking nothing away from any other love.'

~~~~~~~~~~~~~~~~~~~~~~~

Following Lonán's death I stood in the conservatory he built for us. I missed him dreadfully as I looked out over the garden he had loved when I felt him come up behind me putting his arms around my waist as he often did so I leaned back against his chest in happiness.

It was wonderful to feel him close, to feel his arms around me until I remembered... 'he was passed on!

In the moment of realization that he was physically gone, I had to save myself from hitting the floor!

I was surprised shocked and delighted and in awe 'all at once' that he had come back to me; if only for a moment.

It was amazing to feel him 'his complete being.' His energy and the reassuring comfort of his arms around me again as if he was letting me know that our parting would not be permanent.

We all transcend towards our own spirit level of loved ones after physical demise.

It's a part of the perimeter of our spirit being.

There is much outside of this perimeter yet we are always part of our own level of spirit soul family group interrelations within the magnetic 'energy of our love connections'

I feel blown away so to speak by the frequent beautiful events of late loved ones unexpectedly appearing right in front of me as I go about my daily routines since having my dying returning experience.

Then again at other times I am aware of an absolute overwhelming loving energy within the personality of a particular late loved one being near me, usually on my left side.

Such an event happened just yesterday as I was about to reach up to the shelf of my wardrobe where I needed to retrieve a present I had for the birthday of one of my granddaughters.

Totally unexpectedly I felt the presence of a late much loved cousin. A cousin who had been more of a sister than a cousin to me throughout our childhood.

I whispered a simple 'hello' and felt her presence move away.
There are few such beautiful experiences of pure love like this in this life.

~~~~~~~~~~~~~~~~~~~~~~~

Heart Sent From Heaven

Sometime later as I sat outside in the garden that Lonán loved so much, I was feeling sorry for myself so I sent up a prayer.

Lost in my grief I stared down at the patio/driveway bricks he had laid 'when a perfect heart shape water vapour mark appeared out of nowhere!' It was there for such a long while that I managed to photograph it on my mobile phone before it faded away. I keep the photograph on my bedroom wall; sometimes I move it to my bedside table.

Above is the photograph I managed to take of the heart shaped water vapour mark I saw on the ground in front of me as I sent up a prayer while my heart broke with grief over missing my beloved Lonán.

Lonán's Extraordinary Events

Lonán spoke to me of two profound paranormal events which he experienced long before he and I met yet both were similar to my own.

The first one took place when he got home from the funeral of his much loved second wife called Ginger 'her nick name because of her beautiful red hair.'

Undoing the knot in his tie, he was about to walk into his bedroom to change out of the suit he wore for the funeral when he saw his Clara in the doorway blocking his way!

What are you doing here Pet, he said, he would often call the women he loved or liked Pet 'we just buried you!'

Her mouth didn't move but he heard her lovely voice say 'I'm alright' before she faded away!

The next happening took place twelve years before he and I met.

Having just made himself a cup of tea which he was about to take into his sitting room 'he loved his tea' he found himself falling to the floor the tea spilling out everywhere!

The next thing he remembered was waking up in alarm to find himself laying on the floor.

However he must have passed out again because the next thing he remembered was waking up for a second time to find the kitchen in darkness.

Managing to get up from the floor and succeeding to make some more tea he took himself to the bedroom only to find himself falling face down onto the bed, tea spilling out everywhere, this time all over the bed.

The next thing he knew he was up in the corner of the bedroom with his arms folded across his chest looking down on his body sprawled out over the bed 'thinking to himself I do feel sorry for that poor sod down there!'

He knew nothing more until he awoke to discover himself in a hospital bed and that he had been operated on for bowel cancer and gall bladder removal. He still longed for that cup of tea! Eventually one was brought to him by his nurse.

~~~~~~~~~~~~~~~~~~~~~~~

Unforgettable Happenings

When Lonán fell ill for a second time I was busy looking after his needs when on one particular afternoon a dearly loved friend whom I hadn't seen for some time was standing at my side!

I was so surprised but as I was busy hurrying to attend to Lonán's needs I put it out of my mind only to notice my dear friend standing to the left of me again.

I felt such love emanate from him which was so wonderful but then as I watched 'he faded away!'

The shock of all of this stopped me in my tracks so much so that I had to sit down.

I didn't say anything to Lonán as he was so very ill at the time however he did notice something had happened because he said 'slow down, stop rushing around Pet!'

I thought this visit meant that my dear friend had died but a couple of years later I discovered he hadn't died at all when he came to my side but had gone into a coma at that time.

I can only surmise that his visit to me may well

have taken place during a 'near death experience' which he might possibly have undergone while he was fighting for his life in a coma at that particular point in time.

A few months or so before my beloved Lonán and I met I was on my way home following a visit to see my late brother.

I carried a heavy suitcase with me as I tried to manoeuvre myself across a very hazardous road on the way to my travel connection point.

As I waited for a lull in the traffic I noticed a sweet nicely dressed old lady with pleasing well groomed honey and slightly grey coloured hair attempting to cross this busy road alongside of me.

Eventually we managed to cross safely and strike up a conversation as we fell in step together. The lady informed me that originally she was from England but on marriage had settled in her late husbands country.

On finding we were both heading for a nearby coffee bar we continued to pass the time of day where she went on to tell me about an experience of hers that was similar to my own NDR.

Her story was so remarkable that I hung onto her every word.

Regrettably I didn't have the time to tell her about my own dying event because I was clock watching, I didn't want to miss my coach connection.

This is her story...

One morning while in her kitchen (just as Lonán had been in his kitchen when he had his paranormal experience) she was about to pick up her kettle when she felt a strong sharp pain in her head she then felt herself falling to the floor.

Her next memory was of finding herself outside her home as she stood alongside several of her neighbours all watching an ambulance blare out its warning siren to other motorists as it drove off down the street away from them.

Turning to one of these neighbours she asked what was happening but received no answer so she put the same question to another but again no answer came!

Feeling slighted she moved on to more of her neighbours. All of whom knew her well but to her dismay she was completely ignored. In bewilderment and despair she sent up a silent prayer as she turned to go inside her home but as this dear lady was about to go inside her house she found she was now 'inside' the very ambulance she had just witnessed speeding off down the street!

Not only that but now she found herself looking down at her own body from above it!

A young male paramedic stood at the side of her body doing his best to revive it.

Then without warning she felt herself go right back into her body!

This upset her greatly because she had felt much happier above it so in anger she shouted out in utter frustration at the young bemused startled paramedic.

Shouting at him in no uncertain terms that she wanted to stay where she was even if her neighbours were ignoring her because she felt so good out there and up above her body!

By the time the ambulance arrived at the hospital she felt relaxed and resigned to her situation but guilty about her outburst so she apologized but the young man told her she need not worry about it because he was quite used to sick people telling him weird things!

A week or so later I was looking through some books in the pre-loved book store of the seaside town where I had first met my late beloved husband.

One book in particular caught my attention, its subject was an investigation into the paranormal but as I reached out for it someone else managed to grasp hold of it before I could reach it.

I turned to see who this was and found myself looking up into the face of a tall lovely young woman with beautiful long blonde hair.

Oh I was interested in that book I said because I've experienced more than a few paranormal happenings of my own.

She just smiled and headed off towards the cash desk, completed her purchase and left the store.

I browsed through a few books then left the store myself.

Once outside I was surprised to find her waiting for me.

The young woman asked if she may have a word with me. I nodded agreement and in a quiet polite manner she proceeded to tell me about an amazing paranormal experience which she had recently experienced.

I found her story riveting!

Wow I thought; in view of my own experience as well as the story I had been told just over a week previously I wanted to hear what she had to say.

This was her story.

While travelling in the car she shared with friends; she was asleep on the back seat when the car crashed.

One minute she was in the car then the very next moment she found herself to be peacefully outside of it on the sidewalk, feeling very happy serene and carefree...

... and particularly engrossed in the immense enjoyment of the beauty around her.

Nothing seemed to matter to her apart from the overwhelming warm rays of an extraordinary gorgeous and unusual sun that shone down on her upturned face on what was a sweet appealing summer day.

People bustled around her going about their business, ignoring her which was somewhat confusing to her.

Being 'a head turner' this may not have been something

this lovely girl would have been used to but then... in the blink of an eye, she found she was looking in through the passenger window of the car she had been travelling inside just a few moments ago and there on the back seat she 'saw herself!'

The young lady went on to tell me how oddly unconcerned she felt about this fact as she brimmed over with a wonderful carefree calm freedom and happiness at the way the lovely incredible strange sun shone down on her face!

All this made her feel safer than anything she had ever known, she felt free and so good!

The car sustained devastating damage yet even this left her unperturbed!

Then in the very next moment she found herself back on the opposite side of the sidewalk amongst the same crowd of people continuing to ignore her as they went about their business yet all that mattered to her was the incredible beauty of the day which still overwhelmed her!

Feeling fully determined to take full advantage of the enjoyment she felt she continued to stay in the beauty around her until suddenly she was overtaken by surprise to find herself moving on into the inside an ambulance!

Where she was shocked to find herself looking up into the faces of two perturbed paramedics struggling to put a breathing mask on her face which emphatically she did not want!

Adamant that she was not going to allow the mask to be put over her mouth she tried to fight them off because above all else she wanted to stay outside where she felt so good free and happy!

So angry and upset with the paramedics was she that she screamed some really pretty unseemly language at them for bringing her back into her body against her will.

Afterwards she felt so sorry for her behaviour so just as the sweet old lady had done, she too apologized!

As she was abroad journeying home to England at the time I do not know if those paramedics understood what was being said to them but from what was related to me I feel they most definitely would have recognized her anger!

I am left in awe over the fact that in the space of a week or so 'two separate and very different kinds of people' relayed accounts of their own personal yet very similar experiences to my own.

What was so amazing too was the fact that I was to meet these strangers who each in their turn thought it fit to single me out to relate these events of theirs that had taken place so recently in their lives.

To my mind this fact is amazing given the rarity of such experiences as well as the fact that I had also died and come back however my experience was somewhat different in that I journeyed on further into and through a vortex.

Having said goodbye to the young woman I meandered on down the street where I met up with an acquaintance of mine who was a sweet well dressed lady about ten years my senior, refined in manner.

Today the clothes she wore were of a soft blue.

I was so overwhelmed by what I had just been told that I decided to convey these details to this acquaintance who listened to me in polite silence.

When I finished speaking her reply took me by surprise not just because of its content but the casual way in which it was given!

Oh yes she said, 'sometimes the shock of an accident like that can temporarily separate the spirit soul from the body!'

This was said as though the information was very ordinary indeed but I had never heard the like of it before and the more I think about her words the more they make sense to me.

I was not to see the lady again.

I heard she died soon after that chance meeting of ours.

~~~~~~~~~~~~~~~~~~~~~

The Spirals!

Just before the surprising unexpected 'catapulting' out of my body I saw many 'spirals in front of my eyes, like the one below.'

I assume this was due to a lack of oxygen getting to my brain.'

An oxygen deprived brain goes through stages of dying; in my case one of them seems to have been the 'seeing of spirals.'

~~~~~~~~~~~~~~~~~~~~

'I knew' I was seeing these spirals from within my brain, not from outside of it.

Astonishingly a short while later I found myself being 'catapulted out of my body and then looking down over it!'

On investigation I have since learned that 'the phyllotactic spiral pattern forms a class of patterns within nature and general development biology.'

So maybe it is not a surprise to have felt and seen its patterns as my brain entered its first stage of dying.

My 'DCB' experience has not just given me a sense of 'peaceful knowing that life does not end, 'it just changes form' but it has also opened up for me an interest in the science of metaphysics.

[I heard the meaning of what I am about to say mentioned by a gentleman called Andrew Bennett recently on a 'U Tube Ted Talks'... 'Abracadabra, a saying we used a lot of when I was little to portray a magical surprise but what it really means in the original old Aramaic language is... 'What I speak is what I create!' words create the emotional environment we live in.

Help from A Dying Uncle

Words can produce an environment of love kindness and joy or hate spin 'lying deceit' and it's done just like that... 'Abracadabra... instantly!'

I know this to be true in my case I have 'satisfyingly' and 'sadly' created both on occasion so have experienced the truth that most of our thoughts have the power to create reality; sooner or later.]

Thinking back over my life I realize there were many episodes when I would stop breathing, always during damp or frosty cold early mornings

During those times I 'felt myself float up to the ceiling and back into my body again' so maybe due to these small out of body events maybe this is why I experienced occasional paranormal events because it does seem to be that OBE's can open up a portal between spirit mind and our brain that is normally closed off.

Each one of my children and I almost died while I gave birth to them. With my first born I felt we both may have died momentarily; this may explain why we may have been open to 'seeing my uncle's spirit as he relayed an important message to us when we found ourselves in a desperate situation, in need of help.' This is about...

... the occasion I am about to relate. My young husband and I found ourselves stranded with our young baby and small child one miserable dismal wet evening with nowhere to turn.

We needed somewhere to stay overnight urgently but we couldn't find a vacant bed and breakfast establishment motel or hotel so we decided to split up and meet later at an agreed rendezvous.

Hubby went on ahead in the hope of finding overnight accommodation for us while I proceeded to take the opportunity to feed and change our baby as well as comfort our little girl who was showing signs of tiredness before heading off to find a bus pick up point to get us to the agreed rendezvous.

The evening had turned decidedly chilly. A light rain had started to fall. I instructed Celeste to hold on tightly to the handle of the stroller but her harness was already connected for extra safety.

As we walked she sang to herself just as I used to do when I was her age. Baby Ricard lay sleeping in his stroller quite oblivious of his surroundings and the chilly damp evening air but he was wrapped up cozily 'as snug as a bug in a rug' as they say.

We walked for a couple of hundred yards when little Celeste began shouting excitedly... Look Mommy there's Uncle 'On the bus, On the bus!'

Look Mummy, she kept repeating over and over and so I looked up through the rain to see a red bus slowly ambling along close to the sidewalk, its speed matching our walking speed.

The bus was like those big red London 'two deck types.'

Passengers were squeezed together like sardines in a tin so to speak; people were standing in the isle of the lower deck and there in one of the window seats nearest to us sat my very own Uncle waving his hands in an urgent attempt to get my attention.

As I met his gaze he began to mouth something to me but I wasn't able to make out what he was trying to say.

Undeterred he carried on mouthing the words until 'with

relief on my part finally I understood.' He was advising me to go to the home of his eldest son, my cousin, mouthing out the address to me until 'I got it.'

Then smiling he gave us a goodbye wave of the hand, the bus picked up speed and sped off over the brow of the hill until it was out of sight.

As we stared after it Celeste asked when we would see Uncle again. I assured her we were going to see him soon because that is what I fully expected.

I did wonder what he was doing out of his area because you see 'as far as I knew he should have been hundreds of miles away.'

Once safely aboard our awaited bus I took the opportunity to jot down the address he relayed to me.

It would have been nice to have had the use of mobile 'phones back then, sad to say very few working class households even owned a land-line.

When hubby and I met up he was in a distressed state of mind; Kady he said, in a frenetic frustrated tone bordering on panic, 'absolutely everywhere I looked is fully booked because there's a big festival in the city tomorrow.'

What are we going to do he asked as he picked up our bags then answering his own question he said, 'we could get an overnight train to somewhere then travel back in the morning that way we'll be dry and we might even get some sleep.'

A good idea of his I thought but as soon as I could get him to listen to what I had to say he calmed down.

Suffice to say we made our way to the address Uncle had relayed to me and were given a huge welcome that was beyond mere kindness; something I will treasure forever.

If it were not for my dear uncle giving that address to me I dread to think how or where we would have spent that night.

The next day I discovered the fact that my dear Uncle could not possibly have been on that bus that evening because he was in a hospital bed hundreds of miles away and very ill, he died soon after.

I can only surmise that due to the pain and trauma of his illness, the soul (spirit) part of him may have left his body and been somewhere

Angels in Disguise

between this world and the next.

The following event took place three days after giving birth to my first child.

Having gone through three days in labour and then moved by a police escort from one hospital to another to give birth by caesarian section I lay alone on a bed inside a private room feeling very lonely and in pain.

Then another three days went by but my baby had not been brought to me so I was pleased when the door of my room opened to reveal a pleasant sweet looking woman.

Approaching my bed she explained that she had come to help with my pain as she was the ward physiotherapist.

The lady didn't touch me at any time as she instructed me on how to move myself over onto my side without pulling on the metal stitches just below my tummy button.

When I felt pain wash over me she asked me to concentrate on the handle of the wooden door opposite my bed and as I did this she said all my pain would subside which it did.

I felt such kindness emanating from the woman.

Her presence was comforting, helping me to feel less lonely by giving me the feeling that I was well worthy of her attention and loving care.

I soon drifted off into a pain free sleep.

When I awoke I felt rested composed and unworried.

A few minutes later my beautiful little baby girl was brought to me.

Later I asked that my thanks be given to the ward physiotherapist for the help she had given to me only to be told in an abrupt manner that they did not have any ward physiotherapist!

Over the years I have often thought of that lovely lady especially if I'm in pain.

At those times I concentrate on her and imagine that door handle and again I feel her love and peace wash over me.

I see her lovely face in my minds eye to this day even though it's been a long time since that day she came to help me. The memory of her stays imprinted on my mind. Nowadays I wonder if she was some kind of an Angel sent to bring comfort as an answer to any prayer my dear mother who often sent up prayers on my behalf may have said for me.

Another event that stays in my mind is that of a mysterious lady who appeared at my side one day as I went about my daily routine.

The rather sweet pretty woman asked if I would be willing to meet up with her the following day as she had something she felt she must give to me, she then moved away and was gone.

I was intrigued of course but my life was a busy one so I didn't have time to dwell on the matter.

The following day I decided to cycle rather than walk. When I reached the spot where we had met the day before 'there she was holding out a book to me.'

The subject of the book was about people of all ages who had died touched Heaven and returned, 'just as I had done!'

Later I was to learn that the book given was one of the very first to be published on the subject of near death experiences.

Although my experience was more one of actually 'dying and coming back' rather than a 'near death' experience.

I looked for the woman often afterwards but was never to see her again.

The book was a great help to me because it gave me the encouragement I needed to open up to others in respect to my own experience.

I often wondered whether that lady was an Angel or someone 'inspired by an Angel' to bring the book to me.

~~~~~~~~~~~~~~~~~~~~~

Cross in the Clouds

Not long after dear Lonán passed on I looked up and saw this 'cloud cross in the sky. It appeared very significant at the time because we had just sung a lovely old traditional hymn he loved called...

...'The Old Rugged Cross, at his funeral!'
I felt this was a message of comfort from him for me.

Foretold in Every Detail!

What I wish to write here is about something that happened fifty six years ago now but it has been on my mind ever since.

Early one morning as I was preparing to go off to work for the day...

... I heard Mom's footsteps on the stairs; she then walked on into the kitchen where I was sat at the breakfast table.

Mom let out an odd deep sigh pulled back a chair and sat down opposite me looking visibly shaken. I felt alarmed by this as I waited for her to speak.

This was par for the course in those days, 'giving deference to one's elders' and I was well schooled in that respect.

Finally she said 'Kady something very odd strange and upsetting happened to me this morning.'

Seeing her distress I got up from my seat took a cup and poured out some strong tea adding a little more sugar than usual then I pushed it gently across the table towards her before sitting down again, 'I was a little on edge because I didn't want to be late leaving for work.'

I hoped the tea would calm her, this it seemed to do then in a moment or two Mom related...

'...I swung my legs out of bed and was just about to slip my feet into my slippers when I saw something strange loom up in front of me on the bedroom wall opposite the bed...'

I saw she continued, 'a hearse covered with freshly picked daffodils intermingled with lovely tiny white flowers, 'Mom went on as though she were talking to herself 'as if I wasn't there.'

It looked like a television screen but without any casing surrounding it she said,' [this was way back in the nineteen sixties when televisions were bulky; the screens were usually surrounded by heavy wooden casings...]

The grass beneath the feet of the pall bearers was rich green with small explosions of daffodils scattered about.

Above the hearse I saw a large black cross and big black lettering that showed the date, day of the week 'Wednesday' and the time 'twelve - o - 'clock Midday!' Then the scene faded away!

I tell you Kady she said, I felt scared. I could see she was visibly shaken. 'It must be a warning sign she mused to herself.'

I felt sorry for Mom because I knew I would not like to have such an experience as seeing someone's funeral on the wall like that, as if it were real!

Mom took note of the message given in what I now call some sort of holographic vision by taking it as some sort of a warning, foretelling the death of my (gratefully) absent father.

However this turned out not to be so because this experience of hers 'of seeing what she saw on her bedroom wall that morning' was actually the foretelling of her very own funeral!'

Which took place at precisely 12-clock midday on a Wednesday.

Mother's mahogany hearse was covered with freshly picked daffodils intermingled with tiny white flower*s*.

The grass beneath the feet of the pallbearers was a rich green with small explosions of scattered daffodils here and there!

~~~~~~~~~~~~~~~~~~~~~

So my dear Mother was shown an actual vision of her very own funeral which was precise in every detail except that it did not show in which year it would take place.

Her funeral took place exactly twelve years after her vision!

To my mind I feel it was unfortunate that my beloved Mom didn't or was not able to relate this precognitive vision to herself. If she had done so I feel sure she would have made better decisions for herself and her family.

Maybe most of us would not like to know when we will leave this physical life but since my dying experience I think I would be grateful to know so I could focus my own decision making better.

Having said that this may be because I know 'and know that I know' without any question the fact that although there is biological death there is no such thing as the death of me, 'my inner being.'

I know consciousness is more than my biological brain because of the fact that after catapulting out my physical body I was a separate conscious me!

I have never known such happiness as I knew after dying and entering the tunnel like vortex where quiet serenity flooded into my spirit mind!'

I felt more alive and more myself too and my thoughts were crystal clear; my whole self felt fresh and full of energy.

I did not expect to die and so I did not go through days weeks months or years of sickness leading up to death.

I 'shot out of my body so unexpectedly that I don't think my mind had time to realize any beliefs I may have learned over the years of my life, religious or otherwise So thankfully my mind did not 'play out' or materialize any dying brain scenarios.

I had experienced more than a few out of body happenings where I floated up to the ceiling and was able to look down and be pulled back into my body but always during some of my asthma attacks.

During those experiences I felt and knew I was still very much my physical self and I would always go back down into my body yet when my body actually died I knew beyond any doubt whatsoever that 'of course' I was no longer a part of my biological body!

Before dying I had absolutely no idea that I would shoot out of my physical self then go through a tunnel like vortex or see mist or colours or use telepathy or become part 'though temporarily' of the consciousness of my children!

'I am sure such knowledge would have freaked me out!'

I had no expectation of the things that happened to me or the things I saw as I travelled eagerly through my stunning protective vortex...

... such as the wonderful expanse of deep space or the beautiful earth like planet I almost reached before I was 'about turned.'

The belief I held very strongly from childhood was that I would be 'waiting for the last trump to be sounded when Jesus returned in the last days of earth. I would then be resurrected from the grave 'if I had been saved by accepting Him as my personal saviour.'

Otherwise I would not be resurrected, I would be lost along with the millions who lived before the physical Jesus or those who have never heard of him but this did not happen to me.

To me above everything the mission of Jesus and The Buddha was the teaching of compassion and kindness 'above all else' towards all fellow humans and all living creatures and not just of course, within the self delusion of self righteous religious verbal-ism...

... because compassion and unselfish kindness especially under the stresses of life 'more especially poverty or in the other extreme an excess of riches' is our greatest lesson so we can grow our inner soul through such experiences.

[Such considerations of thought have been on my mind lately but just in theory form seeing as it now transpires that human kind have resided on this earth for many millennia, far longer than the mere 5,000 years I was brought up to believe...

... did humanity sustain losses of spiritual and physical knowledge as well as a loss of a lot of human and animal foods now lost to us due to nuclear destructions which caused the ancient yellow desert glass that only come about by nuclear destruction. Is this why meat eating came about?]

Wars including nuclear ones happen because unlike

Heaven 'where even though free will is also de-rigueur' here on earth we live out our lives without the fellowship of telepathic ability.

Telepathy is an automatic ability once we leave the biological sphere of our mortal brain.

Needless to say 'if we had telepathic ability this would be a very different world.'

Naturally of course Lies greed and deceit cannot be hidden in a telepathic world but...

... we would not learn such profound soul gaining lessons that come only from experiencing a fickle good/bad society.

~~~~~~~~~~~~~~~~~~~~

Angel Music

Not so long ago I had an extraordinary experience when out of the blue I began to hear the most beautiful music I have ever heard in my life.

I didn't know where it was coming from so I asked my eldest son Ricard if he had switched a radio on somewhere in the house even though I knew that if he had done it would have been out of character for him.

No Mom I haven't he said, 'shall I play some for you, what would you like to listen to?'

I told him it wasn't necessary because I could hear music in my head! 'He must have thought I was crazy!'

Eventually I acknowledged the beautiful music was only being played out in my mind so because I couldn't do anything about it I had no option but to remain calm relax and take comfort and strength from the soothing tranquility it brought to me.

Such a moving experience that totally overwhelmed me.

I continued to hear this lovely music for twenty four hours of every day for seven whole days and I noticed that when I tried to concentrate solely on the music it would stop until the awful agony of my pain would draw my focus back towards it then it would start up again!

Gradually I learned to simply go with it 'let it carry on in the background of my mind' which was good because it helped me to drift off to sleep or even to think about other things.

On day seven of that week I felt a lot better and as the day wore on the music grew fainter and fainter, by the time the day came to a close the music was gone!

By then I wanted it to stay! Those seven days of illness were traumatic for me but the beautiful gentle soothing music gave me strength to cope and a knowing that 'a Guardian Angel was helping me to get through all that pain.

~~~~~~~~~~~~~~~~~~~~~~~

Guardian Angel

There are two childhood events of mine that stand out in my memory.

The first happened when I was about six years old; I fell off the bottom step while trying to climb onto a bus which I was used to travelling on quite frequently and alone too; I doubt that would be allowed nowadays.

I remember staring transfixed by the big black wheels bearing down on me but not being able to move.

Then I felt strong hands pulling me out and away from those wheels so close to me!

The conductress who noticed me fall off the step jumped off the moving vehicle grabbing me thus putting herself halfway under the bus too and we rolled away together in the nick of time just as one of the back wheels was about to go right over me!

Once safely on the curbside I looked up at the conductress and then up at the other faces of the passengers crowding around us.

[I was so proud of the new red check gabardine mackintosh coat one of my favourite aunts had bought for me but far from pleased when it's clumsiness and weight hindered me under the bus!]

I remember feeling scared and alone despite the grown up people around me until I heard a comforting voice from somewhere close by say 'all will be well for you now.'

I looked around but I couldn't tell where the voice came from. Nowadays I wonder if that was the voice of a kindly person or a Guardian Angel.

My second experience also involved myself and a bus.

It took place around the time my baby brother was born.

He was born at home at a time when mothers were obliged to stay confined to a bed for two weeks after giving birth.

This was during a cold late December. Icicles hung from the rooftops as well as on the trees.

The snow on the ground was icy and it was getting dark as I remember on the evening I witnessed my mother crying because Father's supper was accidentally ruined; there's nothing else in the larder suitable that I can serve up to him, she sobbed.

This was just after World War Two so rationing was in force but fish and chips were unrationed 'if available of course.'

As I watched her tears I felt upset too knowing how angry Father could be.

I was quite used to running errands and travelling around on our local buses so I confidently volunteered to take the bus to our local fish n chip shop but Mom was reticent until I reminded her that we did have a bus stop outside our house and it stopped right outside the shop!

After some thought Mom agreed to let me go and proceeded to help me on with my coat hat and my gloves and then wrote out her note of request for the shop's proprietor whom mother knew well and he always had a big smile for me.

Tucking the money required inside the note and slipping it into the right pocket of my coat along with the penny I would need for my fare Mom put my penny fare for my return journey into the reasonably deep left pocket of my coat and off I went quite confidently at the appropriate time to catch the bus feeling very important and proud of myself. [Even at that young age I loved to 'have a purpose.']

Mom stood in our open doorway until she saw I was safely on the bus.

Everything went like clockwork but I had done this journey many times though not when it was dark outside.

My purchase completed I left the shop with my father's supper under my arm crossed over the road to wait for the bus for the return journey and found quite a queue of people already waiting there.

Eventually it arrived.

I wasn't last in the queue but it was the polite custom for school age children to wait until the grown-ups boarded first in those days so I was the last to attempt to board however before I tried to do so I put my hand into the left pocket of my coat to retrieve my penny fare but it was gone!

I fumbled around every centimetre of that pocket but it wasn't there! I tried the other pocket too but it wasn't there either.

I glanced up at the bus driver who looked annoyed with me for taking so long to board so I turned on my heels and ran off. The bus moved away.

[In retrospect I feel sure my fare would most certainly have been waved given the circumstances.]

As I slowed into a walking pace I realized I had a steep hill ahead of me. The cold was bone chilling but the lovely warmth from Father's supper was so comforting against my chest but by the time I reached home the food had gone cold.

This worried me because I knew Father might be angry if it was served up cold and I worried about the scolding I would receive for losing my fare.

However when I stepped indoors Mom greeted me with grateful relief because I was safe.

Helping me out of my coat hat gloves and shoes she hung up my coat slipped her hand into its pockets and as she did so there in the left pocket where she had put it 'was my penny!'

I stiffened as I waited for the expected scolding but apart from a most enquiring expression on her face it did not come!

The following morning our pleasant natured neighbour 'Peggy' asked Mom if she had heard about the bus that skidded and rolled backwards down the hill turning over onto its side, the previous evening? Mom hadn't and it was the very bus I should have been on!

As I was a small child I most probably would have been thrown about inside the vehicle causing serious injury or worse.

I overheard Mom telling Peggy that she thought maybe a Guardian Angel had been sent in answer to her prayers for my safety by preventing me from finding the penny so I wouldn't take the bus!

I wondered over this because I really searched that pocket as well as the other one and there was no penny to be found!

As a child Lonán fell under a bus too, a London bus when he was around thirteen years old but he ended up in a hospital for a couple of weeks.

Sad to say two of his toes had to be amputated which ended his dream to continue playing soccer for his school that term.

Residue of a Heavenly Visit

Nowadays I find that I often see and feel the spirits or if you prefer 'the souls' of loved ones and friends as they pass on and...

... I understand, knowing something of the incredibly beautiful initial events they experience at the start of their afterlife because of my own experience, albeit seems to be that no two journeys into the next world are exactly the same.'

I do hope my next after biological life experience will begin where I left off which was 'almost home in that beautiful world that loomed up in front of me at the end of my vortex!'

I've seen visions of the babies that were to come into our family and I have seen other 'always pleasing paranormal events' although this gift seems to have left me now I am of a more advanced age.'

NDR has given me great comfort because I now have no fear of dying and it has given me the knowledge that after this life is over for my loved ones friends and beloved animals we will still be together within the other reality we go back home to 'beyond the stars.'

To my mind it seems that because of and following on from my dying/returning experience 'a part of my mind has been opened to things from the world my spirit experienced after the brief death of my biological body.'

I did not realize this is what I was at the time but I was 'absolutely the ghost' of my physical self on the morning I underwent my 'dying/returning event as I looked down over my dead body.

Sometimes during other asthma attacks I often left my body involuntarily and temporarily by…

…'floating up to the ceiling and then gently back into my body again'…

… so I literally became the 'ghost of my body on those occasions too.

Warning from Heaven!

A memorable cousin of mine now passed on, had an amazing dream one night in which she saw her beloved late step father banging on her bedroom window...

...this couldn't have taken place in normal circumstances because the bedroom was very high up from the ground...

... his loud insistent banging awoke her to a strong alarming smell of smoke so she got out of her bed and rushed to the top of the stairs where she saw flames coming from the kitchen!

It's a scary thought that if it were not for that warning dream she her husband and their family may have died in their sleep that night.

It's uplifting to know that my late beloved cousin's much loved step father who is also the beloved uncle whose spirit ghost imparted information to me that I had no way of knowing 'is still looking over his family even though he graduated from this life many years ago!'

It seems to me that some people are looked over and even rescued 'if it is not their time and or if it is possible for them to live out their lives or a further portion of their life here on this earth in some measure of safety but if not then things are allowed to take their course.

In these circumstances love and comfort awaits during and after physical death.

Due to the beautiful dying experience I had and then to come back I decided to look at the experiences of others on this matter.

Although I find my experience does have strong similarities with most other afterlife experiences mine seems to have been quite different too.

For instance I did not go through the life review that other experiencers say they had but maybe I was turned back before my life review could take place.

Yet I knew within myself 'my being, my spirit, my soul mind,' [although I do not know how I knew] but 'I did know' I had entered the great law of a karmatic state of being!

Although I felt very safe and free within an environment that had my best interest at heart.

There is an automatic law which could be called 'Karma' which ensures...

... we go through the same suffering pain hurt and emotion we deliberately inflict on others without remorse on our part while in this life.

Not a comfortable thought but I also felt I was 'inside a caring love for me!'

From research I've carried out it seems we are shown a panoramic view of how our life panned out here 'all the good and the bad bits.'

Apparently no-one judges us because all judgement comes from within our own spirit. This is probably the greatest judgement of all because you see 'any deliberate hurt' caused to others puts our own soul inside the pain of that same hurt during our life review.

I know karma is no 'respecter of persons' and I knew from the beginning of my journey through the sure-fast safety of the beautiful vortex that everything has great purpose.'

Living for a time in a biological world is for us to learn and thus grow through varied experiences. It might be that by failing 'to learn' could be an explanation for reincarnation.

One part of knowledge that has stuck in mind from my dying/returning event is this 'spirit souls who habitually refuse to abandon their own abusive egotistical controlling mindsets borne out of learned political and even religious ideologies are automatically storing up a lot of 'after physical death sorrow' within their own being 'by their own choice.'

It's an immutable fact or law which our spirit soul does know. Does understand regardless of the spirits goodness or lack of it after biological death.

Consistent indulgence of evil leaves an imprint within the soul and harms the spirit soul mind itself far and above the harm it has caused to its victims 'be they animal or human.'

Victims heal and move on to new life levels of loving spirit growth 'post death over in the twin world we call 'Heaven'

Sadly the ever persistent perpetrator automatically put itself into the minutiae pain of the abusive hurtful crimes it has executed on others during this life 'after leaving this life itself.' I understood this within my conscious spirit a few moments after entering my vortex yet I also knew I was 'safe.'

Needless to say it's not possible to prove my experience because spirit life cannot be quantified or put into any biological measurement or term in this 'our physical world' because nothing of spirit or soul life can be pinned down or 'held onto by the human hand or eye!'

Unless one's physical brain is given the profound experience of it of course but even then one cannot grab it in the hand and show it to others.

~~~~~~~~~~~~~~~~~~~~~~

The next chapter is the startling telling of something that happened to me just a few weeks ago.

Something completely 'astounding.'

Merging Souls - a Love That Refused to Die

This chapter is difficult to write because I still reel with shock from a most remarkably phenomenal event that has given me a stunning feeling of comfort and great joy but...

... I don't know how to begin. I feel the tears welling up in my eyes now as I type.

Friday had been quiet and once again this happening occurred just when I was about to watch my brand new television through my brand new fire stick!

This time the evening news was due to start.

I set a cup of freshly made tea down onto the coffee table and was just about to settle myself into my rather low armchair when I realized a person from my past, someone I had loved dearly whom I hadn't seen in forty four years (and that was just a brief few minutes) 'stood right in front of me!'

I stared in pure shock and surprise as I heard myself say 'oh Jal!'

By the time I sat down 'Jal' from decades ago had stepped right through my body 'merging us into one!'

As Jal came through my body I felt such love filling up every particle of my being!

I have not felt such incredible love as that before and neither have I ever felt anything so beautiful.

I felt every centimetre of his essence as he became 'one with me!'

Never have I known any other feeling on this earth to compare with the ecstasy of those few moments of time.

The sense of 'oneness with Jal filled my whole being with incredible comfort and happiness that took my breath away!'

This was someone I was very close to and had grieved over for decades.

Tragically our relationship was cruelly thwarted when malicious lies by letter besmirching Jal's character ensured steps were taken to completely remove me from the situation so that any possible contact between us couldn't take place.

'So sad when a jealous envy 'as in this case' sets itself out to destroy the life intentions of respectable people.'

Mi Cariño

If only mobile 'phones were in use in those days then such a separation would not have taken place.

Yet now in spite of all that, out of the blue to have experienced the happiness of Jal and I merging together as we did means we have finally come home to one another in a way I could not in my wildest dreams have ever imagined!

I assumed Jal 'mi cariño, mi cielo... my love, my Heaven' must have died and crossed over into our next reality of being which seems likely yet...

... there is the possibility that he visited me while in a coma or in an altered state of consciousness which could well occur in cases such Alziemers where it seems possible for some sufferers to experience a near death event where the inner spirit soul or attached consciousness leaves its physical body and is then drawn towards whomever or wherever its thought wishes to be.

Whilst it's been well over fifty years since we were together we had such a strong connection in that 'he was my home' so I have thought of him every day of those years and often wondered how his life had gone.

However I could never have expected his soul, spirit or whatever it may be called to find me and merge with my being!'

This means he did not forget me or our love.

I feel comforted elated and honoured by the experience since it means that despite the maliciousness done to keep us apart for no good reason except jealousy the fact is 'love between two souls does not die, it continues post physical life.'

It's heartening for me to know in absolute truth that the love between Jal and I had lasted through the decades for both of us which means that one day in the not too distant future our spirits will reunite again within the world of our newest reality where we will resume our merging to walk through all the memories our love held...

... regardless of what was done to us in this life!

The Great Consciousness corrects all soul injustices once we return home to the safe world of del Cielo 'of Heaven.'

~~~~~~~~~~~~~~~~~~~~~

Initially the 'merging experience' filled me with great elation but after an hour or so the fact that I had felt every tiny centimetre of Jal's energy as it passed through me brought back such deep memories of having him physically near me that I went into the shock of severe grief.

I missed him so much, as well as the years we had lost out with each other.

After a couple of weeks or so of this overwhelming grief I realized I needed to remember the most important thing of all about this experience 'which is...

... in the end the love between Jal and I couldn't be destroyed by lies injustice or time because our spirit souls reunited and we will reunite again over in the world we call heaven.

So... while our separation here was forced upon us we can look forward to the happiness of merging again once my time here is done.

I do not know where Jal is, whether he is still here trapped in a sick body or whether he has passed on but I think it is more likely that he is back in his spirit form.

'After all the hours and years of feeling adrift I have the assurance of knowing that a new time will merge us once more over in the afterlife but firstly I have to wait 'por ahora...for now.'

A strong pull of love contains within it a magnetic spirit DNA that is never blotted out even if there may have been friction this side of life.

There was never friction of any kind between Jal and I.

My merging event with Jal's soul was far beyond any connection lovers feel this side of life.

Of course I take nothing away from any other loves Jal may have known in this life 'and vice versa in my life here' because the part of his heart that belongs to me and the part of mine that belongs to him 'is what will always be ours.'

It's incredibly consoling to me to know that after physical death the spirit can find itself close to those it loves who are still here regardless of 'where' that person may be in the world at any particular point in time!'

~~~~~~~~~~~~~~~~~~~~~~

Jal had no idea where I lived yet his soul found me!

The DNA of love is composed of some sort of 'magnetic energy.'

I was able to go to each of my grown up children on the morning my body died albeit temporarily and...

... my spirit found them 'I became part of them' although I might add that not in the same way as my long lost love merged with me as the experiences with my children were more on an emotional mother child level.

Equally my late beloved friend had no idea where I was to be found when he appeared at my side, indeed I could have been in any part of Europe yet his spirit soul was able to find me!

I must say my beloved late mother could not have known exactly where I was to be found either because I had moved several times since she died yet her spirit found me!

I had moved house too several times after my late dog had died yet her little spirit found me!

When I found myself with each of my children when I catapulted out of my dead body I didn't decide to find them or go to them, it just happened!'

After the death of the physical body love automatically unites as if by magnetism with its twin love and loves.

The soul cannot rest without love. Love is an amazingly powerful 'element of electric magnetism'... an energy whose DNA is 'love.'

Final Thoughts

It was difficult to be coming back through my vortex and heartbreaking for my spirit soul consciousness but I knew I couldn't leave my small child if it were possible to go back.

I felt such concern too for my grown up children as they wouldn't understand how I could die so suddenly as well as the fact that they wouldn't know that I 'myself was safe and in a good place.'

I knew we would all be together in a spirit soul family one day but I was new to being just spirit so the pull of my little boy and closeness to my grown up children 'was raw.'

This to my mind is understandable considering how suddenly I was 'ousted out of my body!'

Having metamorphosed into a spirit soul it all felt natural and normal except for the fact of 'looking down at my lifeless body, it was very strange and eerie!'

Before I died I frowned on religious beliefs I was not brought up to believe.

Now I know how unnecessary in the scheme of 'the after mortal death world' that attitude was.

Religion is just a tool mankind invents to fathom out a purpose for its being, when what truly matters is how we each interact with one other within this earthly mortal life.

The heart of the Great Consciousness 'God' is simply that we learn the lesson of spirit 'that all interactions we may base on lies selfishness and greed only lead to soul unhappiness.' The truth is that our own hands on experience so to speak, can teach us this.

The Great Consciousness never demands or needs worship because it is not that insecure or vain, 'everything is about our souls learning so we grow in the wisdom that integrity and love brings.'

Our journey of learning does not end at all after physical death either; it still takes place according to whatever level of spirit mind understanding we are at.

We do not suddenly change character just because our physical body dies either on the contrary we stay on the journey of soul discovery.

Consciousness is a continuous ongoing changing energy.' The whole universe of course and beyond consists of 'energy'.

We are 'ourselves' made up of energy; an energy that is within us 'attached.'

It stays attached until biological death sends it on its way back to its home.

Without that measure from The Great Universal Consciousness biological bodies of any kind would not work just as a radio or computer cannot work until it receives 'energy from its power source!'

As I departed from my physical body I knew that I had been set free and as I travelled through my post death vortex 'I knew I was going home!' How I knew this, I don't know!

From recent studies I've made into the near death events others have written about, something important runs through many of those experiences.

Those such as my dear late brother who was brought up to fear the Devil because he was told he would end up with the Devil when he died because of the bad deeds done in this life so often they retain a deep fear up to the moment of dying.

So sad when grownups determine to terrify young minds like this. I remember being told I would see the Devil if I looked into a mirror too much!

In my late brother's case, this fear resided within his subconscious mind twenty four hours of every day.

He was considered a difficult child because of his many temper tantrums but I now realize how his anger was brought about because he would often be accused by the grown-ups of doing things he was often innocent of.

At other times 'children being children' it was because certain family members would antagonize him on purpose so as to make him angry as well as pointing the finger towards him for misdeeds they themselves were guilty of doing.

Sadly he took to the taste of alcohol in his young adulthood becoming alcoholic along with the smoking of cigarettes yet he believed these things to be a sin 'along with card playing' but to indulge in such things were reportedly sins of the Devil. This is what we were taught.

Such ingrained beliefs brought horrible regular nightmares for him 'all about the Devil, more especially if he had drunk alcohol' and more so because of his low tolerance to it but other people of course who may have positive beliefs may see and gain comfort from seeing their beloved leaders rather than the Devil as the mortal brain dies just as a television/radio etc., receiver diminishes when it's power is slowly withdrawn.

In cases like this it does not surprise me at all when it is said that the dying brain sees subjective beliefs play out as they die and rise above the body...

...some do not go past this point because they find themselves back again in their physical body either because it is...

... not their time or they may choose to come back as in my case or it may simply be due to modern resuscitation methods.

However once the spirit soul has moved on passed the initial first stage of dying then they find they are heading towards a world of upper spirit reality, towards the level of the world of Heaven their subjective growth of soul has attained.

[I remember feeling emotionally moved at the bedside of a friend of mine dying from a long term illness as he reached out in reply to his deceased loved ones and his late Mom just a couple of days before he died.' I felt they came to give him the comfort he needed.]

In my case before my dying returning event I held the belief that Jesus or the Devil would greet me after I died.

Depending which it would be I would either end up in hell or see Jesus and then be asleep in my grave until the last trump is sounded when Jesus returns to earth and the dead 'those who died in Christ by accepting Him as personal saviour' would then have their graves opened and be resurrected to meet Him in the sky.

This did not happen to me! My dying brain didn't materialise this maybe because I catapulted out of my body 'as fast as a fired bullet' with no expectation of dying.

I'd had difficulties with my breathing in the past but the problem always abated so as usual I expected it to stabilize at any moment however this time was different because I suddenly shot right out of my body and wow it was a very strange feeling! 'Not scary though.'

A kind of resurrection without a wait in the grave. I have no fear of physical death instead I long to graduate from this life into the next world to the level of soul reality that my spirit understanding has attained where amazing beauty and new experiences and learning take place.

We live out a life here in a trying environment where egoísta 'self' is tested.

I'm sure I was put to the test when I reached the end of my vortex when told 'this need not be your time.' I could have been selfish and given in to my own need to stay in my beautiful attained level of the afterlife but I decided out of love to come back.

My strivings here can be challenging because I continue to learn tough lessons via my personality failings.

If acts of altruism take place under the heavy pressures of this life to be selfish it will lead to satisfaction happiness and integrity for our spirit soul consciousness.

At the end of the day when ultimately I move on from life in this world I hope I will have given out more kindness than I did unkindness.

This is the message of all the great teachers such as Jesus and Buddha.

Kindness does not mean martyrdom as that would be a negative drain on us but a beneficent frame of mind puts us into a nicer journeying into the world we all came from... the world and the Great Spirit we all go back home to.

It makes no sense to care or worry about what others thinks of me anymore because all that matters to me is to finally graduate from this life with more spiritually positive marks than negative strikes.

When again I speed on through the vortex 'only God and I my soul spirit' will know which is which.'
The Great Spirit Universal Consciousness is everything to us 'mother father sister brother and all those who give us love' but most of all a friend.'

[Footnote... When we are born into this life we accept everything around us as normal even though we find everything fascinating so it was after I died I accepting everything that was happening around me as normal even though I found it very fascinating!

No longer can I subscribe to the saying 'God will not give us more than we can bear' because everyone has free will so there can be 'no hold on the wickedness some people do to others and to the animals in their care' but little do they know that they themselves will re-live... will experience within the spirit soul that same hurt that was done deliberately during life here 'while experiencing the life review after physical death.' [I found it comforting to know 'that when suffering becomes too great to bear just before physical death the spirit mind mercifully leaves the body.'

'A sobering thought this... 'the quality of the person we have allowed ourselves to become before we leave our physical body is the quality we take into the world we call Heaven and the level we will find we get to once there'... and I did not lose my own individuality after my body died as I think Buddhist's believe I should have' instead I found my spirit soul body was still very much individualistic while I was a part of something greater, something that was a beautiful oneness with other beings.']

' The Life we Live… is a Life… But…

it is Not the Only Life we will

Live.'

Printed in Poland
by Amazon Fulfillment
Poland Sp. z o.o., Wrocław